oo fat? too thin?
the healthy eating handbook

Crabtree Publishing Company

www.crabtreebooks.com

Crabtree Publishing Company
www.crabtreebooks.com

Author: Dr. Melissa Sayer
Editor: Molly Aloian
Proofreaders: Adrianna Morganelli, Crystal Sikkens
Project coordinator: Robert Walker
Production coordinator: Margaret Amy Salter
Prepress technician: Margaret Amy Salter
Project editor: Victoria Garrard
Project designer: Sara Greasley

With thanks to Dr. Sarah Schenker

Every effort has been made to trace copyright holders, and we apologize in advance for any omissions. We would be pleased to insert the appropriate acknowledgments in any subsequent edition of this publication.

Picture credits:
Getty Images: p. 25
Sara Greasley and Hayley Terry: front cover (bottom),
    back cover (bottom), p. 6, 8, 10 (top), 13 (bottom),
    15 (top), 17, 23 (bottom), 26 (top), 28 (top), 32 (top),
    38, 41 (top), 42 (top), 44 (top)
iStock: p. 1, 12, 26 (bottom), 28 (bottom), 30 (top),
    32 (bottom), 34, 36
Shutterstock: p. 2, 4, 5, 7, 9, 10 (bottom), 11, 13 (center),
    14, 15 (bottom), 16, 18, 19, 20, 21, 22, 23 (top),
    23 (center), 24 (top), 24 (bottom), 27 (top), 27 (bottom),
    29, 30 (bottom), 31, 33, 35, 37, 39 (top), 39 (bottom),
    41 (bottom), 42 (bottom), 43, 44 (bottom)
ticktock Media Archive: front cover (top),
    back cover (top)

Library and Archives Canada Cataloguing in Publication

Sayer, Melissa
    Too fat? Too thin? : the healthy eating handbook / Melissa Sayer.

(Really useful handbooks)
Includes index.
ISBN 978-0-7787-4392-7 (bound).--ISBN 978-0-7787-4405-4 (pbk.)

1. Nutrition--Juvenile literature. 2. Body image--Juvenile
literature. 3. Eating disorders--Juvenile literature. I. Title. II. Series:
Really useful handbooks

RA784.S378 2009   j613   C2008-907913-2

Library of Congress Cataloging-in-Publication Data

Sayer, Melissa.
    Too fat? too thin? : the healthy eating handbook / Melissa Saye.
        p. cm. -- (Really useful handbooks)
    Includes index.
    ISBN 978-0-7787-4405-4 (pbk. : alk. paper) -- ISBN 978-0-7787-
4392-7 (reinforced library binding : alk. paper)
    1. Nutrition--Juvenile literature. 2. Body image--Juvenile
literature. 3. Eating disorders--Juvenile literature. I. Title. II. Serie

RA784.S392 2009
613--dc22
                                                2008052554

Crabtree Publishing Company
www.crabtreebooks.com   1-800-387-7650

Published in Canada
Crabtree Publishing
616 Welland Ave.
St. Catharines, Ontario
L2M 5V6

Published in the United States
Crabtree Publishing
PMB16A
350 Fifth Ave., Suite 3308
New York, NY 10118

contents

introduction

Think of a female celebrity. Any one will do. She has been in a magazine with "Too Fat"? or "Too Thin"? written next to her. Guaranteed.

Some celebrities are too thin one week and too fat the next.

Lily Allen has been labeled too thin and too fat by different magazines in the same week. Are these the people we're supposed to look up to! OK, forget the celebs. Even normal people are concerned about body size 24/7. Headlines. Talk shows. Even debates in government. Sometimes it feels like we're all going to bust from obesity. Or snap from anorexia.

Did you know?

Every person is made up of about fifty trillion cells. This book will make you feel better about every single one.

What really matters?

- Wouldn't it be great if it didn't matter about fitting into skinny jeans? Or having a six pack?
- The truth is, we often focus too much on these things—and not on what's really important, like eating right and feeling good.

Here's your honest, no-nonsense and airbrush-free guide to staying sane in a body-conscious world. Find out:

how to eat right
how to look after your body so that it looks and feels great
what to do when you're not happy with your shape
and best of all, how to accept your body

how's your body image?

Body image means how we see ourselves and how we feel about how we look. Take this quiz to discover your body image...

When I look in the mirror I think...
a) Not bad, could look better—but I'm OK.
b) I am totally fabulous!
c) I hate my body and I hate looking in the mirror!

After a day shopping for clothes I am...
a) Happy—I've found some clothes that suit me.
b) Desperate to get back out there—so many clothes, so little time...
c) Miserable, nothing looks good and I wish I were a different size.

You've just finished this week's celebrity magazine. Are you:
a) Irritated. These people are so perfect! You'll cancel your subscription.
b) Hysterical. Celebrities try so hard but look so bad!
c) Upset. You'll never measure up.

You jump on the scales and find you weigh 2 lbs (9.5 kg) more than you expected.
Do you think...
a) It's time to try harder. I really should quit the snacks.
b) Chin up. Who cares?
c) My whole day is ruined.

What goes through your mind after a big family dinner?

a) "Mom's apple pie is so fattening, why did I have thirds…?"

b) Nothing, except "Why is it always my turn to wash up…?"

c) "I feel guilty and bloated. Why can't I stick to salad?"

If you could change one physical thing about yourself would it be…

a) Your belly or thighs. Or maybe your height.

b) Not a thing—I am fine the way I am.

c) Everything could be better, especially the wobbly bits.

Answers:

Mostly As

You feel insecure at times and wish you looked different. But mostly you resist the pressure to measure up to an impossible standard. You just get on with being you.

Mostly Bs

Here's looking at you! Wow! Your confidence and security is enviable. How do you do it? Try and be patient with those lesser mortals who fret about their body image.

Mostly Cs

It seems your body image is pretty negative. You spend a lot of time fixing on an impossible standard and feel bad because you aren't perfect. Go easy on yourself. Try and spend at least a day a week where you forget all about your body and just relax.

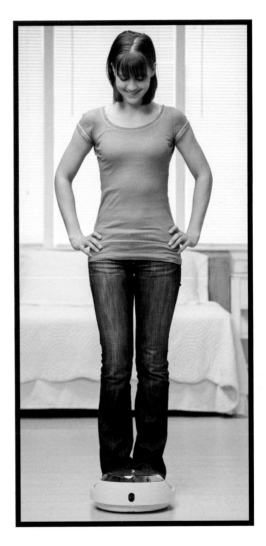

I hate my body!

A negative body image is not about being vain or a perfectionist. It's about having low self esteem and feeling insecure.

What we say

- "Beauty is only skin deep."
- "It's what's inside that counts."
- "Don't judge a book by its cover."

What we think

How we look seems to be more important than anything else:

- Around 80% of ten-year-olds are afraid of being fat.
- The average age dieting starts is eight.
- Young girls are more afraid of being fat than they are of nuclear war, cancer, or losing their parents.
- Men may think about sex, on average, every 20 minutes but women worry about their weight and body shape every 15 minutes.
- Two out of every five women and one in every five men would trade 3–5 years of their life to achieve their ideal weight.

We risk our health

- Many women have taken **laxatives** or slimming tablets. These cause damage to our bodies which can be fatal.
- Many women have tried fasting.
- Many women exercise excessively to lose weight.
- All of the above threaten our health in the short and long term.

We splash our cash

- Americans spend over $40 billion on dieting and diet related products each year.
- Think about what we could do with the money we save.

Why do we do it?

- Everywhere we turn, there are pictures of perfection. Models and celebrities on every billboard, TV station, and magazine. Even if we think they are dumb, the message is clear: to be important and successful, it seems you have to be thin, toned, and beautiful.
- Even if we are happy with our bodies, studies have shown we become less so after being shown TV ads featuring exceptionally slim and beautiful people.
- Experiments show that seven out of ten women are more depressed and angry after looking at pictures of fashion models.
- It's not just the girls. The pressure on boys to be picture perfect is just as bad.

time to get positive

So celebrities are seriously bad for our health. But before you reach for that diet plan or get on the scales, again, hold up..

Here are the official four questions everyone with a negative body image must ask themselves.

1) What does a celebrity have that I don't?

- Staff, including personal trainers, stylists, cooks, and make-up artists
  They don't do it alone.

- Cosmetic surgery

- Airbrushing
  No one looks that good. It's impossible. Don't believe your eyes. Just ask any photographer.

) Who are the important people in my world?

Do you hang out with your best friend because her thighs are toned? Do you love our dad because of his six-pack? Why do we rate body image in ourselves, when . is not so important in other people?

) What about poverty?

s it really OK in the 21st century to be so hung up on a tiny bit of **fat**? Half the world (three billion people) live on less than two U.S. dollars per day?

) What are all the things I am good at?

Your sense of humor. Great smile. These things are much more real. And important!

Let's all agree it's time to quit...

- sighing whenever we squeeze our thighs
- feeling miserable when we're in the changing room
- thinking we're uncool without a six-pack
- believing the hype: celebrities aren't all they're cracked up to be

Instead of beating ourselves up, we should take a look in the mirror and be proud. Aren't we looking hot just the way we are?

puberty and body shape

Did you know our whole body shape changes during puberty?

Puberty facts

- We know about the hairs, and the genitals. Half of us get the breasts and the periods, too. But there's a lot more to puberty.

- Puberty starts around age 10 for girls and 11 for boys.

- Any time between 9 and 14 is totally normal.

- It lasts about three to five years. In that time, we will grow taller by up to 10 inches (25 cm).

- We will gain 15–55 lbs in weight (7–25 kg).

Big or small?

he size we end up depends on our:

Genes. Look at your mom and dad. If your parents are tiny it's unlikely you'll be playing basketball professionally. Sorry.

Eating habits. If we eat a healthy, **balanced diet** (see page 38) we will grow to our full potential.

Health. I'm not talking about the odd cold or tummy bug. Being unwell for a long time can slow our growth, making us end up slighty shorter.

Did you know?

When asked what they would do differently if they had their teenage years over again, many adults said: "Not worry so much about how I looked…"

size zero

Size zero is tiny. I mean really teeny weeny. So small that most clothing shops don't stock it.

What is size zero?

- It's so small that nearly everyone is bigger than size zero when they start buying adult clothes. We go through our natural size zero phase at age eight.

- Size zero is the freakish celebrity who looks like she'll snap if she bends over. Whose head is too big for her shoulders. Who seems to have spent the season surviving a famine. I'm serious. One magazine was fundraising for African women. They were bigger than the size zero models on the fashion pages.

Size zero hits the headlines

- The organizers of Madrid Fashion Week banned models with an unhealthy BMI (less than 18 see page 24) from their catwalks in 2006.

- In 2007 a model named Luisel Ramos died of a heart attack at just 22 years old. She had been living on green leaves and diet coke for months.

- So size zero is not just an impossible, unhealthy example for women and girls. It's downright dangerous for the models themselves.

The truth about size zero

The U.S. dress size 0 = UK size 4

31.5 inches (80 cm) (bust)

23.5 inches (60 cm) (waist)

34 inches (86 cm) (hips)

The waist size is that of the average eight-year-old.

But if I put my mind to it, can't I be a size zero, too?

- Size zero is safe for less than two % of women, based on their height.
- For everyone else, striving for size zero means, at best, misery, mood swings, and endless hunger, and at worst infertility, heart failure, and even death.
- Pass the Kit Kats!

obesity

Simple to explain, right? We eat more than we need. Period. Do that for long enough and we become obese. No big mystery.

But why do some people become obese when others don't?

- Genes have something to do with it. We are dealt a hand at birth. Some of us can eat more than others and not put on weight.

- Others seem to look at a cream cake and they are piling on the pounds. This is because their bodies are better at storing extra **calories**.

- Scientists think the obesity gene gave a survival advantage to our evolutionary ancestors. Lay down fat in the summer when crops are plentiful and you would survive the bitter winter with little or nothing to eat. Watching your slimmer cave-dwellers drop like flies.

But is this the whole story?

No. Not even close. Even if we are born with the tendency to be fat, we only become so by eating more than we need.

So the real question is: why are we all eating so much?

Over to you:

"We are all large in our family. Helpings were [bi]g. We thought we had healthy appetites. [O]ur mom loved to cook and eating was a [bi]g deal. It was only when I started having [sl]eepovers with my friends that I realized [ho]w much extra we actually ate."

"I started eating more and more when I was bullied at school. The more they teased me for being fat the more I ate. I hid food in my room and comfort ate, trying to cheer myself up, I suppose. It just made me feel worse. The fatter I got the more shy I was and the worse I ate. It was a vicious circle."

"I don't think I eat a whole lot, really. No more than my friends. I am sporty and I swim all the time. It's so not fair."

Is obesity a problem?

After all, curves are beautiful, sexy, and gorgeous. And if you are truly happy with yours, maybe it's better to stay that way than beat yourself trying to achieve the impossible. Trouble is, people with obesity have more to deal with.

- We are more likely to be bullied and suffer from low self-esteem and **depression**.
- We get out of breath doing exercise and our joints hurt when we try.
- We are much more likely to get heart disease, high **blood pressure**, **diabetes**, and even some cancers. So we are more likely to die young.

diets: the good, the bad, and the ugly

Anyone can lose weight. Stop eating and it comes off. The hard part is doing it right.

Healthy dieting means:

- we don't miss out on all the fun stuff our friends enjoy
- we don't put the weight back on the moment we're off our diet
- and above all, we don't get ill trying

But it's not easy

"I've tried every diet under the sun. It all goes well for a bit but as soon as I stop the diet the weight piles back on."

I eat when I'm stressed and tired. After a difficult day, all my good resolutions go out the window. And if I've done well at something, I treat myself to chocolate on the way home."

"It just seems such a mammoth task. It means months and months of saying no to my favorite things."

So why is it so hard to eat right?

Quitting unhealthy eating is one of the hardest habits to break. Imagine giving up cigarettes, drugs, or alcohol. We can avoid our habit. Stop buying them. Or hanging out with people who do. We just say no. But we cannot give up food. So temptation is there, 24/7. We can't avoid it, every single meal time.

Fad diets

Fad diets like The Maple Syrup or Cabbage Soup diet are popular. There is no food to think about. No temptation. And the weight falls off. Big mistake.

• If we try these extreme diets and eat fewer than 1500 calories per day, our body switches into starvation mode. Our metabolism slows right down. As soon as we eat normally our body stores the calories as fat. In case the hard times come again. Long term result? Weight gain.

Fad diets don't teach us to change our eating habits for good. So we end up resorting to bad habits (miss breakfast, snack, pig out in evening) all over again.

We only know we've quit over-eating for good if we can eat normal stuff, same as everyone else. But just go easy on the portion size.

diet dilemmas

When it comes to dieting, it's all about getting the balance right.

"I can't start eating different things from the rest of my family. My mom gets upset if we don't clean our plates and ask for seconds."

It's time to get the family on your side. To succeed in anything we need the support of people around us. Explain how you are going to do this right—slowly and healthily. Offer to help with the shopping and cooking. Your mom will come around. She might even join in...

Isn't it harmful to try to lose weight when you're still growing?

Drastic weight loss can be harmful at any age, especially if we're still developing. Before starting on a diet, ask for advice and support from your family doctor. They may suggest you aim to control, rather than drop your weight. As you grow taller, you'll even out. As long as you're eating a healthy balanced diet, there's no age limit to eating right. Set yourself up for life.

ere's your top tips for achieving (and keeping) a healthy weight

❯ Exercise burns calories. It also speeds up our metabolism so we continue burning more, even when we've taken our running shoes off. We may even get hungry less often and full more easily.

❯ Fruit and vegetables are full of goodness and easy to fill up on but low in calories. Make sure you get at least five portions per day.

❯ Oats are low calorie and high **fiber**. This means they fill you up and keep you going for hours without getting hungry again. Pass me the porridge.

❯ Snacks. Everyone likes to snack so make sure your fridge is full of stuff like carrot sticks and apples. A handful of peanuts has the same number of calories as five apples!

❯ Portion size. There is no reason why you can't have your cake. And eat it. Just be careful not to supersize your meal. See page 22.

Did you know?

Most people cheer themselves up with food. It starts when we're little and given sweets "if we're good." We all need spoiling, but try and find other ways to treat yourself.

Remember

Anyone considering losing weight should speak to their **GP** for advice and support first.

portion size

Roughly how much is a portion?

Carbohydrates

Eg. pasta, rice

One portion = size of clenched fist

About one-third of your diet should
be made up from carbohydrates, so
have a portion at each main meal.

Protein

Eg. meat or fish, beans, eggs

One portion = size of deck of cards

Cooked beans = half a cup full

Egg = one

Have a small portion with each main meal.

Dairy

Eg. cheese, milk, yogurt

Cheddar cheese (one portion) =
size of matchbox

Milk = one glass

Yogurt = one small container

Choose low fat varieties.

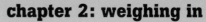

Fruit and vegetables

Eg. apple, banana, peach

One portion = one piece of fruit

Or a large handful of grapes or berries

Or a cup of chopped vegetables

Eat at least five portions per day

Butter

One portion = size of half an index finger

Shocked? I know I was.

We might think all we've eaten is pasta. But when the bowl is overflowing to the size of a fist wearing a boxing glove, we've actually eaten five portions of pasta!

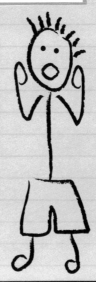

BMI

Is our weight all that matters?

The right weight for us depends on our height. Our BMI is a measure of our weight, in relation to our height.

Imagine 140 pounds (63.5 kg). This is a lot for a Kylie Minogue, height: 5' 0" (1.53 m). And about right for a Rhianna, height: 5' 8" (1.73 m). But much too little for a Steve Redgrave, height 6' 5" (1.96 m).

Here's how to work out your BMI

BMI = your weight in kilograms, divided by your height in meters, squared.
For example, if you weigh 65 kg and you are 1.68 m tall, your BMI is 65 divided by (1.68 x 1.68) = 23.

What does my BMI mean?

<18.5	Underweight
18.5–24.9	Healthy
25–29.9	Overweight
30+	Obese

If your BMI is not in the healthy range, our health is at risk. The further outside the range, the more likely your weight is to make us unwell.

The problem with BMI

A word of warning: BMI is not always helpful. Three reasons:

1) BMI figures are for adults aged over 18. Until we've stopped growing, it may be OK to have a slightly low BMI.
2) BMI calculations may be misleading in athletes.
3) Remember BMI is not the whole story.

Try this.
Take Mohammed Ali.
Do the math on his vital stats:
Height = 1.91m
Fighting weight = 94 kg
BMI = 27 = overweight!
But he was fit, healthy, and it was all muscle.

Imagine two friends. Both have BMIs of 22. Perfect, we think. But one is a fitness freak who eats healthy. The other survives on the three Cs: chips, chocolate, and cigarettes. So there is more to life (and health) than our BMI.
It is not the whole story.

how do you feel about food?

Here are three questions to ask ourselves. And some answers that may mean we're messed up about food.

) Is food on your mind most of the time?

"I plan what I am going to eat every day, before I get up."
"I keep worrying about how much I ate yesterday."
"A good food day is a good day. Period."

) Does it get in the way of other things?

"If I eat too much I have to exercise to burn it off."
"I'm running out of excuses for not going to my friend's.
I can't eat in front of her family."
"Christmas is coming: A big family meal. I am dreading it."

) Is it affecting your health?

"My period has stopped."
"I feel tired but I can't sleep."
"I am close to tears a lot of times."

Sadly, few people (especially women) are 100% happy about their weight.
Few eat only when they are hungry and never feel bad afterward.
But this doesn't mean we all have eating disorders.

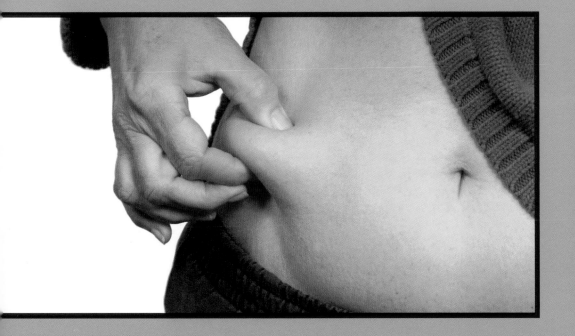

what is an eating disorder?

An eating disorder is when the compulsion to eat or not eat makes us ill. Either physically (body) or emotionally (mind), and usually both. There is a problem when we stop controlling our food and our food starts controlling us.

here are four main types of eating disorders

Anorexia Nervosa

An intense fear of being fat or gaining weight

An abnormally low Body Mass Index (see page 24)

Monthly periods stop or fail to start

Bulimia

Binge eating (uncontrolable bursts of over-eating)

Feeling guilty and out of control about food

Compensating by vomiting, using laxatives, under-eating, or excessive exercise

Binge eating disorder

Similar to bulimia, but with no compensating

Compulsive over-eating

Eating too much throughout the day

Feeling guilty and out of control about food

Many people do not fit neatly into these categories.
We may overlap with more than one type of eating disorder.

could I be at risk of an eating disorder?

Anyone can get an eating disorder. I once met a man in his thirties with anorexia. But there are some factors that might make an eating disorder more likely:

- Being a young woman (aged 15–25)
- Trying to do well at things (a bit of a perfectionist)
- A mom who tries to diet and keep slim
- Having been chubby in the past
- Getting stressed about exams and worrying about grades
- Having a difficult time at home or school

Scary stats

Hundreds of thousands of people in North America have eating disorders.

People aged between 14 and 25 are most at risk.

Girls are ten times more likely than boys to develop anorexia or bulimia.

Over 90% of young people with eating disorders feel unable to talk to anyone about it.

Without treatment, as many as 20% of people with serious eating disorders die.

With treatment that number falls to 2–3%.

How can I tell if I have one?

Doctors sometimes ask the SCOFF questions:

- Do you make yourself sick because you feel uncomfortably full?
- Do you worry you have lost control over how much you eat?
- Have you recently lost more than one pound in a three month period?
- Do you believe yourself to be fat when others say you are too thin?
- Would you say that food dominates your life?

One point for every "yes" in the SCOFF questions. A score of two or more may suggest an eating disorder.

If you have less than two it is very unlikely you have anorexia or bulimia. These questions are only guides. The best way to know for sure is to ask a doctor.

how do eating disorders happen?

For most of us, they happen slowly and gradually. We don't wake up one morning with a problem.

- We might start to lose weight and like how that feels so we carry on.
- Over time, controlling our food makes us feel in control of our life.
- The thought of stopping calorie counting becomes terrifying. Even if we know we are damaging our looks, our health, and our relationships.

It happened to me

"I started cutting out snacks and unhealthy food. I felt better about myself the more weight I lost. So I started to cut down at meal times, too. I'd find ways of hiding food so that it looked like I'd eaten it. I even tried to make myself sick, but I couldn't. Controlling my food made me feel better. I would do anything rather than eat 'normally' again. When I look back, I didn't feel good about myself before I started dieting. I was never cool or clever enough. I guess thinking about food and weight all the time meant I didn't have time to stress about other things."

Emma, 15

I'm worried about my friend. How can I help?

You may notice she's lost weight. Maybe she's talking about diet and exercise more often. She might pick at her food. Or even avoid it altogether. You used to stop at the store on the way home. Now she walks the other way.

Trust your instincts. If you think your friend has a problem, you're probably right.

It is horrible watching a friend get weird about food. I'm guessing you've told her you're worried.

Try encouraging her to ask for help.

Remember it's not your fault she's not eating properly. You can't make her stop on your own.

Be patient. Listen to her when she needs to talk.

And most of all, keep your own eating on track. Don't join in...

getting help

I think I've got an eating disorder. What should I do?

You have recognized the problem. That is fantastic. Some people spend years in denial.

- First, you have to be brave enough to tell someone. Find the right adult and explain what is happening.

- Next, be trusting enough to believe you can sort this out. There is a lot of help out there: experts who know everything there is to know about eating disorders. People who have helped hundreds of people like you get their eating back on track. They are waiting to help you beat this. The best place to start is with your doctor. Ask them for a referral.

on't be afraid to ask for help. It may feel awkward or
mbarrassing at first. But it is the first step back to
eing well.

"I was scared to see the doctor. I thought they'd say I was mental and force feed me. But I saw a counselor and even though it is taking ages, I am getting there."

"I didn't tell anyone because I thought you had to be anorexic before anyone paid attention. My weight was normal but I was messed up about food 24/7. I wish I'd done it earlier."

Most importantly, never forget you are so worth fighting for.
You don't have to live this way. You deserve much better.

food groups

Can you remember everything you've eaten over the last 24 hours? Dozens of different ingredients. The average cookie has at least five.

Across the world, humans must be eating millions of different foods.

Unlike car engines that run exclusively on gasoline, our bodies are able to run on (practically) any food. We can digest it, process it, and use it in some way.

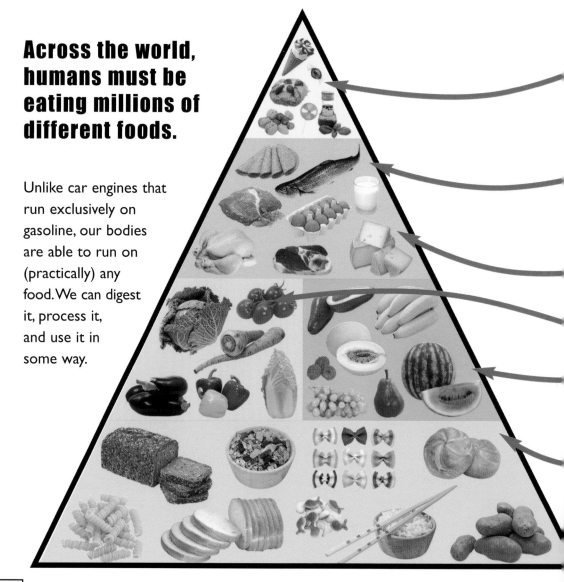

The millions of different foods can be divided into five food groups.

Fat and sugar	**Eat less**
Cake, butter, sweets	
For energy	
Best kept at the end of the list. Eat little.	
Protein	**Eat more**
Fish, meat, beans	
For growing and mending the body	
Try to eat fish twice a week	
Milk and dairy	**Eat more**
Cheese, milk, yogurt	
For strong bones and teeth	
Two to three servings of milk or yogurt daily	
Fruit and vegetables	**Eat more**
For every single bit of us	
Serious **vitamin**s, **mineral**s, fiber, & energy	
Eat at least five portions per day	
Carbohydrates	**Eat more**
Rice, potatoes, pasta, bread	
For energy	
About 1/3 of our total diet should be carbs	

what is a balanced diet?

Our bodies aren't fussy. To look and feel brilliant, all they need is some food from all five groups, every day. A balanced diet means just that. A bit of everything.

It's best to eat mostly carbohydrates and fresh fruits and vegetables. Make sure there's some protein and dairy but go easy on the food and drinks high in fat and sugar.

I thought calories were all that mattered...

- It's not just how much we eat. It's about quality as well as quantity.
- The recommended daily amount of calories for an average active teenage girl is 2,200. It's 2,800 for active boys.
- Think of your daily amount as a bank account. You could spend it all on Danish pastries (about 250 calories each) or use it wisely on a mixture of different foods.
- Invest for the future with a balanced diet.

But my mom does the shopping and she makes burgers and fries...

It is tricky if you're eating different food than everyone else. Time to put on that apron and offer to help. Anyone for chicken tortillas?

Top five tips for healthy eating:

1) **Base your meals on starchy foods** like pasta, rice, and potatoes. And go brown.
2) **Eat a lot of fruits and vegetables.** Get AT LEAST five portions of fruits and vegetables a day. There are 7,500 varieties of apples in the world so there is one out there for you.
3) **Eat more fish,** including a portion of oily fish each week. Brain food.
4) **Cut down on saturated fat and sugar.** Grill, don't fry.
5) **Eat less salt**—no more than 0.2 ounces (6g) a day for adults. Stop shaking it on your fries.
6) **Get active** and try to be a healthy weight.
7) **Drink plenty of water**.
8) **Don't skip breakfast.** No excuses. And a packet of chips doesn't count.

Finally, remember to enjoy your food. A little of what you fancy does you good!

the food lowdown

Ever wondered what they mean by....

...Organic food?

Organic food is made to strict regulations: No artificial **pesticide**s or fertilizers for the crops, no growth hormones or antibiotics for the animals.
The plus side: Organic food may be better for our health, for that of the people who produce it, and for the environment. It may also taste better than non-organic.
The down side: It doesn't last as long (no **preservatives**) and it costs more.

...GM food?

Genetically Modified food is developed by changing the genes (DNA) of the plant.
The plus side: Crops are resistant to pesticide and **insecticides**. They are less likely to rot. This helps them grow better and makes them cheaper to produce. It is particularly helpful in the **developing world** where many people are starving.
The down side: Possibility that the genetic changes will pass into other plant species. The health benefits of eating GM food are unclear.

...Fair trade food?

Fair trade food is made with the welfare of the producers (often from the developing world) in mind.
The plus side: It ensures a fair price is paid to the farmers. They can grow crops that will pass from one generation to the next, ensuring their future.
The down side: Can't see one, myself…

What is a superfood?

These are extra healthy foods that may even stop us getting some nasty diseases. There is no ultimate list but most scientists agree on fresh fruit and vegetables, oats, yogurt, nuts, and oily fish (like salmon). Go get yours.

Food facts

- The first ever breakfast cereal was Shredded Wheat.
- There are seven teaspoons of sugar in the average two ounce (60 g) bar of milk chocolate.
- The word cake comes from the Viking word "kaka."

benefits of exercise

Everyone likes curling up with a pizza and a DVD. The couch potato is the best position of the day. But weird things happen to our bodies when it slobs out too much. Obviously, we fail to look like a Beckham. Or win an Olympic medal.

But there's other stuff exercise is good for, too:

Head

xercise boosts our brain power as well as our muscles.
xercise helps us concentrate and think quickly. It also
nakes us happy. Scientists have proven regular exercise is
s effective as **antidepressant medication** when
ve're feeling low.

Face

Glowing, healthy skin. What's not to like?

Tummy

Our insides work better if we exercise. **Kidneys**,
uts, **womb**—the lot. Hands up who gets tummy
ches, period cramps, or constipation? Here's
ooking at you.

Muscles

Our muscles get toned and defined.
Name one athlete who looks bad in shorts.
Darts doesn't count, by the way.

Bum/hips

One hour jogging = 500 calories = four
hocolate bars. That's the kind of math I like.

Bones

trong bones are a given when we're young. But did
ou know the health of our bones in our teen years
nfluences how snappable they are when we're a
ranny? Avoid a zimmer frame in the future.

Heart

erious illness. Heart disease. Cancer. Diabetes.
xercise is like taking out an insurance policy. It
educes our risk of getting these nasty illnesses.
Bottom line: we live longer if we're fit.

get fit

How much exercise should I do?

- To stay healthy, it is recommended that people under 18 get 60 minutes of activity per day.

- That's ten minutes walking to school, 20 minutes kicking a football at lunchtime, 10 minutes home, and 20 minutes perfecting jumping around to your favorite track in your bedroom. Not a problem.

Did you know?

Seven in ten boys, and six in ten girls aged two to fifteen achieve at least 60 minutes of physical activity each day of the week. But two in ten boys and girls are active for less than 30 minutes per day.

To get fit

Adults need 30 minutes of moderate intensity exercise at least five times every week. Moderate intensity means we get a bit breathless and work up a sweat. Take the armpit challenge: a dry pit means try harder.

Did you know?

Around 30% of young people feel negative or neutral about exercise.

The top five excuses for not exercising. What's yours?

"I hate the gym!"
I know what you mean; posers, bad smells, and too many mirrors, but you don't need a gym. Try the park, local swimming pool, or your own bedroom instead.

"I haven't got the time/money."
Exercise for free: ditch the elevator and the bus.
Take the stairs and walk. You don't need designer gear.
If Barack Obama, the most powerful man on the planet, can spare an hour to spend in the gym, then so can you.

"It's boring!"
If after the 200th lap of the pool, you're losing the plot, try varying what you do. Try exercising with a friend. That way it's not a jog round the park, it's a gossip session.

"I'm bad at it!"
Even Cristiano Ronaldo wasn't built in a day. You are better than yesterday.
Go slowly, you'll soon get there.

"I'm too embarrassed."
Going public in our gym clothes for the first time can be like the first day at school. Be proud. Remember, you're already doing better than 20% of the population who never exercise. Chin up.

glossary

antidepressant medication
Medicine prescribed by doctors to help the symptoms of depression

balanced diet A healthy diet achieved by eating from all the food groups in balance

blood pressure The force exerted on arteries (blood vessels) by our blood

BMI Body Mass Index. A number relating our height to our weight

calorie A unit of food energy

carbohydrate Chemical compounds providing the most common source of energy in living things

depression A long term period of serious unhappiness

developing world Countries with low industrialization and often poverty and deprivation for the population

diabetes: A medical condition where the body fails to control the level of glucose (sugar) in the blood

DNA Deoxyribonucleic acid: the genetic material of nearly all forms of life

fat Oily chemical compounds that are insoluble in water and high in energy

fiber The indigestible part of food from plants, which helps defecation (going to the toilet)

food groups A classification system for different foods

genes Units of hereditary information made of DNA

GP General Practitioner, family doctor or primary care physician

guts Intestines, the alimentary canal, through which food passes in all animals

insecticide A chemical which is poisonous to insects

kidneys Organs of the body responsible for making urine

laxatives Medicines which induce defecation

mineral An inorganic material essential for nutrition

pesticide A chemical poisonous to pests

preservative A chemical used to prolong the life of food

protein Biological compounds that play an essential part in the working of our body

vitamin An organic material essential for nutrition

womb Uterus, female internal body organ in which a baby grows during pregnancy

further information

Eating Disorders
www.anad.org/
The National Association of Anorexia Nervosa and Associated Disorders, (ANAD) is America's oldest non-profit organization dedicated to alleviating the problems of eating disorders.

Exercise
www.presidentschallenge.org/
The President's Challenge is an American government program giving tips and support for healthy exercise.

Diets
www.eatright.org
The American Dietetic Association is an organization that provides a wealth of resources for improving your diet.

mypyramid.gov/index.html
The U.S. Department of Agriculture's guide to a healthier diet

Obesity
www.surgeongeneral.gov/ obesityprevention/index.html
For help and advice on combating obesity, visit the Surgeon General's campaign against childhood obesity.

Calorie counting
calorielab.com/index.html
Information on the calories contained in a variety of foods, as well as restaurant portions.

index

Printed in the U.S.A. — CC